DATE DUE

Animal Opposites

BIG

and

Small

An Animal Opposites Book

by Lisa Bullard

consulting editor: Gail Saunders-Smith, PhD
content consultant: Zoological Society of San Diego

Capstone
press

Mankato, Minnesota

Some animals grow as big as an airplane. Others are as small as a speck of dust. Let's learn about big and small by looking at animals from around the world.

BIG

Whales are the world's biggest animals. Many kinds of whales can grow larger than a bus.

Whales can eat millions of krill in one day.

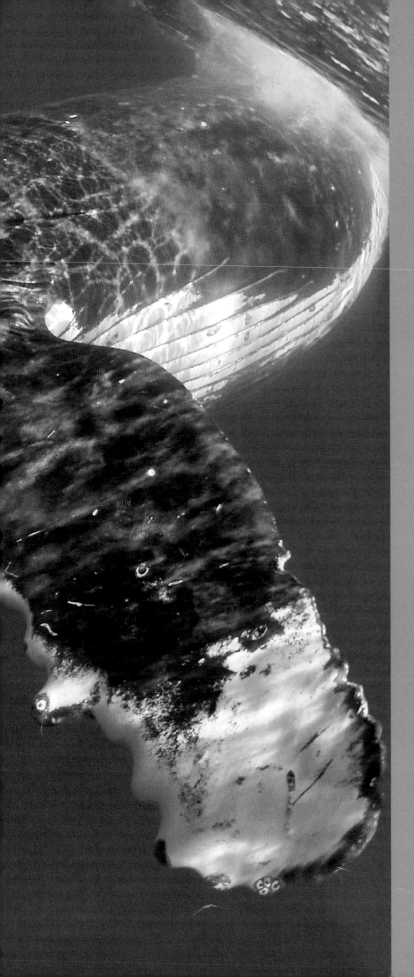

Small

Krill are small animals
that look like tiny shrimp.
They grow to the size
of a person's little toe.

BIG

The world's biggest land animals are elephants. They stand as tall as a basketball hoop.

Small

Small mice live almost everywhere there are people. They even find small places to hide in people's houses.

BIG

Big African buffalo stomp
across grasslands.
They use their large horns
to protect themselves
from lions.

Small

Small oxpeckers eat bugs off larger animals.
They treat African buffalo like fast-food restaurants.

BIG

Big tigers are dangerous hunters. They roam through forests and swamps looking for other animals to eat.

Small

Don't be fooled by a tiger beetle's size. These small bugs are very good hunters.

Tiger beetles move quickly to catch food. They eat crickets, ants, and other bugs.

BIG

Crocodiles are the biggest reptiles around. Some grow as long as minivans.

Small

Crocodile newts aren't
tiny reptiles. They're
small amphibians.

13

BIG

Ostriches are the biggest
birds in the world.
They're too big to fly.

Small

Hummingbirds are the world's smallest birds. They're small enough to fit in a child's hand.

The smallest type of hummingbird is about the size of a bumblebee.

BIG

A big male moose grows
new antlers every spring.

Small

Some small animals gliding
from tree to tree aren't birds.
They're flying squirrels.

Flying squirrels don't
really fly. They glide using
flaps of skin between
their front and back legs.

BIG

Big polar bears hunt and play in the snowy Arctic.

Small

Arctic foxes are small but tough. They often eat polar bear leftovers.

In summer, an Arctic fox's fur is gray or brown. It turns white in winter.

BIG

Elephant seals are big and fat. Their blubber keeps them warm in cold water.

Elephant seals are mammals. They need to breathe air. But they can hold their breath underwater for about two hours.

Small

Small rockhopper penguins waddle about the cold Antarctic.

BIG

The world's biggest lizards are hard to find. Komodo dragons live only on some tiny islands in Indonesia.

Small geckos use trees
and rocks as hiding places.

BIG

Big sharks are dangerous
hunters of the deep.

Small

Small, colorful clown fish swim in coral reefs.

Clown fish hide among sea anemones. Sea anemones have poisonous stings that harm most fish. A special coating on a clown fish's skin protects it from the stings.

Some big animals swim in oceans.
Others stomp across the ground.

Some small animals hide under rocks. Others fly through the air. What kinds of big and small animals live near you?

Did You Know?

The largest whales, blue whales, have very big hearts. Their hearts are the size of a small car.

Not only are ostriches the world's biggest birds, but they lay the world's biggest eggs. Ostrich eggs are about the size of a cantaloupe.

Some male polar bears stand up to 10 feet tall and can weigh 1,500 pounds.

Geckos live on every continent except Antarctica.

A mouse's tail is almost as long as its body.

Small clown fish eat bigger fish that sea anemones kill with their poisonous stings.

Glossary

amphibian (am-FIB-ee-uhn)—a cold-blooded animal with a backbone; amphibians live in water when young and can live on land as adults.

Antarctic (ant-ARK-tik)—the area near the South Pole

antlers (ANT-lurz)—bony structures that grow on the heads of moose, deer, and elk

Arctic (ARK-tik)—the area near the North Pole

blubber (BLUH-bur)—a layer of fat under the skin of some ocean animals; blubber helps animals stay warm when swimming in cold water.

coral reef (KOR-uhl REEF)—an area of coral skeletons and rocks in shallow ocean water

mammal (MAM-uhl)—a warm-blooded animal that has a backbone and feeds milk to its young; mammals also have hair; most mammals give live birth to their young.

reptile (REP-tile)—a cold-blooded animal with a backbone; scales cover a reptile's body.

Read More

Bruce, Lisa. *Sizes at School.* Math All around Me. Chicago: Raintree, 2004.

Deegan, Kim. *My First Book of Opposites.* New York: Bloomsbury Children's Books, 2002.

Gordon, Sharon. *Big Small.* Bookworms: Just the Opposite. New York: Benchmark Books, 2004.

Whitehouse, Patricia. *Zoo Sizes.* Zoo Math. Chicago: Heinemann, 2002.

Internet Sites

FactHound offers a safe, fun way to find Internet sites related to this book. All of the sites on FactHound have been researched by our staff.

Here's how:

1. Visit *www.facthound.com*

2. Type in this special code **073684273X** for age-appropriate sites. Or enter a search word related to this book for a more general search.

3. Click on the **Fetch It** button.

FactHound will fetch the best sites for you!

Index

A+ Books are published by Capstone Press,
151 Good Counsel Drive, P.O. Box 669, Mankato, Minnesota 56002.
www.capstonepress.com

1 2 3 4 5 6 10 09 08 07 06 05

Library of Congress Cataloging-in-Publication Data
Bullard, Lisa.
    Big and small: an animal opposites book / by Lisa Bullard.
    p. cm.—(A+ books. Animal opposites.)
    Includes bibliographical references and index.
    ISBN 0-7368-4273-X (hardcover)
    1. Body size—Juvenile literature. I. Title. II. Series.
QL799.3.B85 2006
590—dc22   2004027945

Summary: Brief text introduces the concepts of big and small, comparing some of the world's large
    animals with animals that are small.

Credits

Blake A. Hoena, editor; Kia Adams, designer; Kelly Garvin, photo researcher;
    Scott Thoms, photo editor

Photo Credits

Brand X Pictures, 3 (beetle); Bruce Coleman Inc./E.R. Degginger, 13; Bruce Coleman
Inc./Frank Krahmer, 14; Bruce Coleman Inc./John Shaw, 11; Bruce Coleman Inc./K
McDonald, 12; Bruce Coleman Inc./Kim Taylor, 17; Capstone Press/Karon Dubke,
cover (mouse), 7; Corbis, 1 (hummingbird), 3 (hummingbird); Corel, 27 (clown fish
Craig Brandt, 9; Creatas, 3 (penguin), 26 (whale); Digital Vision, 2 (tiger), 3 (ostric
Digital Vision/Gerry Ellis, 1 (elephant), 26 (elephant); Digital Vision/Jeremy
Woodhouse, 1 (polar bear), 26 (polar bear); Getty Images Inc./Andy Rouse, cover
(elephant); Getty Images Inc./Jonathan & Angela, 8; Getty Images Inc./Peter Webe
23; Getty Images Inc./Tom Walker, 18; Marty Snyderman, 24; Minden Pictures/Flip
Nicklin, 5; Minden Pictures/Tim Fitzharris, 16; Minden Pictures/Tom Vezo, 15; Min
Pictures/Tu De Roy, 22; Peter Arnold Inc./Fred Bruemmer, 19; Peter Arnold,
Inc./Rosemary Calvert, 21; Photodisc, 27 (mouse); Seapics.com/Andre Seale, 25;
Seapics.com/Masa Ushioda, 4; Tom & Pat Leeson, 6, 10, 20

Note to Parents, Teachers, and Librarians

This Animal Opposites book uses full-color photographs and a nonfiction format to
introduce children to the concepts of big and small. *Big and Small* is designed
to be read aloud to a pre-reader or to be read independently by an early reader.
Photographs help listeners and early readers understand the text and concepts
discussed. The book encourages further learning by including the following sectior
Did You Know?, Glossary, Read More, Internet Sites, and Index. Early readers may
need assistance using these features.